]

Random Acts of Kindness are Changing the World

Random Acts of Kindness are Changing the World is a much needed book in our lives today. With so much negativity in our world, Rosalyn has filled this book with stories that will not only leave you smiling but warm your heart to the reality that the most important thing is kindness towards others. You will want to read it more than once.

--Eldonna Lewis Fernandez, MSgt USAF Retired
Award winning speaker, award winning author,
contracts and negotiation expert
www.ThinkLikeANegotiator.com

In Rosalyn Kahn's *Random Acts of Kindness are Changing the World* you will discover the what, the how and most importantly the why of Random Acts of Kindness. She sets the bar for all of to see and act. This powerful book speaks in plain language the goal of leading the life of being in service to others. When we serve others – we serve ourselves. Thank you Rosalyn for this great gift.

--Maurice DiMino
International Speaker, Author and Mentor
MauriceDiMino.com

Random Acts of Kindness Are Changing the World

Rosalyn Kahn

Random Acts of Kindness Are Changing the World

Copyright © 2014 by Rosalyn Kahn.

ISBN: 978-0-9846872-6-8

Primary editor: Joanne Shwed, Backspace Ink
www.backspaceink.com

Editing by Carol N. Hart

Photography by Maureen Benoit

Cover design by JETLAUNCH
www.jetlaunch.net

Dedication

This book is dedicated to my parents Anna and Edward Kahn, who inspired my love for listening and learning.

Next, to my students, who have used the message of kindness to help improve our world.

A huge thanks to all the people who heard these stories and encouraged me to share them with you and the rest of the world.

It is my intention that these stories uplift and inspire you to perform your own acts of random kindness.

Finally, for joining your heart with mine, you have my gratitude beyond words …

*Master the Message with Passion and Purpose.
I am your guide to helping you reach your highest
potential.*

Contents

"We never know the impact that our stories may have on someone else's life."

—Rosalyn Kahn

Foreword

I've always wanted the world to be a beautiful place, filled with gentle and giving souls. I was a teenager in the '60s, awash in the haze and hope of harmony. I'm 60 now, and I still cling to the possibilities of peace and kindness throughout the world.

As I worked with the author, I had the honor of reading real stories of people who were trying to achieve these dreams—one random act of kindness at a time. They came in all shapes and sizes, ages, genders, ethnicities, backgrounds, and social statuses. By doing these random acts and sharing the stories, their lives—and the lives of others—were changed forever.

Through the passion of her words in this book, the importance of Rosalyn's work is apparent. She is an "inner guide," letting everyone know that they can change their world—and, by doing so, change the consciousness of the planet.

I believe that everyone can make a difference. I also believe that whatever I do in my small world affects everything and everyone else. Rosalyn's stories remind me that my behavior always matters, and it doesn't take a lot of time, money, or effort to do a random act of kindness and share it with the world.

—Joanne Shwed, Backspace Ink

Introduction

This book could have just as easily been called *The Conquering Power of Kindness* or even the *Contagious Power of Kindness*. After all kindness really has a unique power all of its own and this force may just be the best answer to so many of life's toughest questions.

Although kindness isn't as sexy as the in your face attitude that most businesses and American cities want to claim as the keys to success, Rosalyn Kahn shows us how so many of the most influential people have been inspired through another's catalyst of kindness.

Interestingly enough, although kindness has a good chance of leading to success, kindness will always lead to happiness. So if you want to be happy, be kind. This book will show you everything you ever needed to know about the power of random acts of kindness.

Random acts of kindness to me is kindness without an agenda. They are service and charity for all the right reasons, which is the highest level of kindness that exists in the universe. (Arguably the next closest thing is secret service or being kind anonymously)

My friend and our author Rosalyn Kahn seems to be one of the foremost experts in kindness, which is the type of attribute that can change businesses, families and ultimately the world. Something truly amazing happens when people start thinking about each other's happiness more than their own. Rosalyn has written about it in a way that has never been read before.

Enjoy!

David T. Fagan
Author of *Guerilla Rainmakers*

Preface
Straight into the Heart

Ever since my youth, I have always enjoyed keeping a diary of life's events. In adolescence, I worked through emotions by writing poetry. Time wore on and the writing became less frequent, but there was always a part of me that loved to put words on paper—even to this day.

Everyone's life has moments of ups and downs where we say, "I should write a book, but I just don't have the time." In a similar vein, there was always a voice inside my head that was determined to come out. I always knew that there was a message I wanted to share with the world but couldn't quite figure out which story I wanted to tell.

I remember that day very clearly: I had finished my college classes in the fall of 2012, and I just gave my first speech on the speaking circuit. In addition, I was interviewing 25 speakers and 25 coaches to figure out how I would map my career to the big leagues as a professional speaker.

One distinguished lady, who ran a speakers' bureau, asked, "What is the focus of your talks?"

I replied, "Well, it could be homelessness, cultural studies, fracturing my wrist ..." and the list continued.

Suddenly, I was interrupted and told, "You will never make it on the stage unless you focus on one area. Call me back when you can spend the time developing that idea."

Little did I know that this would be the spark that helped me find my voice! I frequently receive book recommendations from friends. One suggested Tony Hsieh's book, *Delivering Happiness: A Path to Profits, Passion, and Purpose*. While reading his words and turning the pages, I found that I was taking compulsive notes. Through this effort, I discovered a reawakening of my inner voice telling me to focus on my passion.

I told myself, "I think I have something here. I must share this with the world!"

The content was compelling and the words magically jumped from the page straight into my heart. The feeling moved through my mind like the golden rays at dawn. It was a positive shift in mindset—almost like a blessing.

"Imagine the impact of changing someone's life with a random act of kindness."

This is the message I use to begin a number of speeches. My movement and personal transformation all began with the assignment to simply go out and talk about a random act, and then share the story with my class. Once the words leave the person's mouth, the most amazing things happens.

A "random act of kindness" is a selfless act performed by one or more people who wish to assist or cheer up someone else. Current research in the positive psychology movement shows that we can change the outcome of our mindset by making a choice to choose happiness.

How did I inspire people to act? In *Delivering Happiness: A Path to Profits, Passion, and Purpose*, Hsieh discusses the movement he created surrounding random act of kindness. The history, significance, and magnitude of the movement occurs throughout history. In my classroom teachings, it was a means to an end; for every act they did, they would get the external reward of extra credit points.

It is hard to trace the beginning or end of which story inspired me the most, as each one sets off a different chord in my body and feels that the one being told is the best in that moment. Then, I hear another great story, and the current story replaces the one told before. These stories of random acts began nearly a year ago and every day I am told or receive another random act. These feelings inside my heart are still the same: pure joy and wonder.

Reflecting on my findings with random acts, I found several major themes underlying all of my talks:

Kinder hearts: As audiences hear the stories of the random acts of kindness, they become oblivious to all that has happened before, and inner joy fills their hearts. With the theme of "kinder hearts" in mind, I offer these stories:

- Eduardo, a student whose experiences—beginning with a stranger, moving to senior citizens, and then returning to serve the world through his job at his restaurant—inspired the opening of a foundation for the homeless.

- Marcus, an 18-year-old musician, who serenaded a hotel lobby just for the love of sharing music
- Nikita, and her colleague Benita, who inspired teens at an inner-city youth shelter to become physically active and bond with others
- Franklin D. Roosevelt, who stayed the course of history to preserve a stable future
- Natana, a pregnant student, who helped the disabled with fresh soup and reorganization services
- Nigela, a pregnant Nigerian woman, who went to the grocery store short of cash and a stranger offered to pay her bill
- José, a 16-year-old, inner-city student, who helped a senior collect her groceries after they had fallen out of the bag
- Kelly, a student who gave a cup of coffee to a homeless man while working at Starbucks
- Lisidea, an Armenian woman, who gave her Thanksgiving meal and old clothes to the homeless, and then donated blood

Stronger relationships across society: Acting as an invitation to the world, the completion of random acts crosses all age groups, races, religions, and creeds. These actions serve to unify the different segments of society through acts that demonstrate our ability to share the world live more cooperatively. This began in one city and moved from west to east, making a worldwide impact. With the theme of "stronger relationships across society" in mind, I offer these stories:

- Juan, who encouraged his high school classmates to respect their elders
- Martin Luther King, Jr., who instilled a dream of unification for all people to work together despite their background, race, or color
- Anita, a 16-year-old girl, whose tragic story of how she lost her father, brother, and cousin to gang violence, and then her nephew to suicide—all in less than three months, drew people closer together by inspiring others to reach out to family and friends sharing their love and appreciation
- Alejandro, a 16-year-old who finally recognized the hardships that his single father experienced while raising him on his own
- Saniya, a young, pregnant woman from Yemen, who opened her home to feed fellow refugees from her homeland
- My own story about how the integration of literature, ranging from Shawn Anchor and Steven Covey, frame my experiences and messages that I share with my audiences
- Brigita, who strived to model the skills her mother taught in corporations in her southern Central European homeland of Slovenia

Better physical and mental health: Our doctors advise us to exercise and practice a proper diet, while random acts of kindness feed our minds. When we fill our outlook with good news, then happiness, calmness, and relief are the immediate outcome. With the theme of "better physical and mental health" in mind, I offer these stories:

- A story of my fractured wrist and how I used it as a metaphor for struggle to help my students overcome their fears of public speaking
- Tanya, a Russian model, who distributed daffodils to fight depression
- Amanda, who helped bring Alan, a depressed student, back to positive living
- Juliet, who, on Valentine's Day, met Francesca, a fellow ballerina, and offered to pay the balance of her bill when her friend was buying a gift for her beloved
- Susie, a student, who brought a homeless man named John to her home to get cleaned up, and then sent him off with a care package
- Ryan, a football player, who was benched with a concussion as just college recruiters arrived and Pablo, who broke his finger in a post-season game and tried to play through the pain, whose stories – sharing their personal frustration and angst - helped others in class by opening a dialogue about dealing with obstacles and disappointment along the path to realization of our dreams.

Increased wealth: The greatest gift beyond any price tag is the one of wealth—not a monetary equivalent but an overflowing of the heart. Happier people find that the simple adage of helping out and uplifting employees can greatly increase profits. Giving people positive encouragement can do wonders to reduce absenteeism and much more. With the theme of "increased wealth" in mind, I offer these stories:

- An innovative strategy, which I established to help English as Second Language Learners obtain transferable job skills
- Candace, a successful West Los Angeles beauty salon owner, who struggled to make a short speech in a business meeting
- Steve Jobs, who gave a Stanford University commencement address on life's lessons
- Jamie, a fellow participant in a business training seminar, who treated a homeless person to a meal
- Avo, formerly a homeless man, who readjusted his thinking and turned his life around by helping business entrepreneurs and countries in crisis
- Gary, who created a foundation in Guayaquil, Ecuador to aid and encourage the growth and development of local leaders in emerging generations
- Ruiz, a natural healer, who used natural oils from indigenous countries to heal people here in America
- Annabellina, a 17-year-old Colombian woman, who offered her life lesson to "just let it go and don't sweat the little things," and who told me about Sergio Garcia, a Mexican-born immigrant, who fought for his right to retain his law degree

- Tazania, a Kyrgyz woman, who fed neighbors from her Central Asian homeland to help alleviate homesickness
- Margie, a pregnant, 22-year-old, international student, who shared food received from food stamps with the homeless

Chapter 1
Teaching Kindness

Everywhere I speak, I bring my passion. Truth has power and energy ignites an inner flame. My audience is awed by these words, and in turn, their passion fills the room.

This is what happened when I gave a speech titled, "How to give a more powerful speech through storytelling." Participants learned that the #1 way to get rid of our fear of speaking is by addressing a topic for which we feel great passion. The topic shared was the work done with random acts of kindness, such as holding an elevator.

One 17-year-old high school student named Juan told his classmates, "We youngsters really need to respect our elders. We will all be old someday!"

Youth today are often given a bad rap for the prevalence of gangs, graffiti, and drugs. Here was a student who was professing the good acts they can do in society. Many other students looked shocked as one of their peers shared his suggestion. My heart was smiling, and I recognized that there *is* hope for our future generation.

Primarily, we are all hard-wired to do good deeds as it makes us feel so good. It's part of a survival strategy shared by all humans. Secondly, we can transfer these positive emotions to others by sharing such good feelings. This inner voice resonated in my heart and encouraged me to share this example with my audience. Our daily newspapers are filled with bad news. It is easy to view the world through this dim view as an ugly and unhappy place. Yet, listening to your inner voice and sharing stories like these brings happiness to others.

It is amazing what random acts can do to change our world. They are both beautiful and effective – a simple act is so easy to perform and yet has great potential to influence attitude and outlook, making a huge difference in someone's life.

One story stands above the others, written by Eduardo. On the very first assignment in my public speaking class, he wrote:

"A lot of teachers give us meaningless activities to waste our time each and every day. Yet, this assignment I know has the greatest value of any I have ever done and wonder what I indeed will be doing on the last speech."

Eduardo is a good-looking, well-built, former high school wrestler, whom you would describe as not easily swayed by emotion. He visited a Starbucks on the way to work and decided to buy a coffee latté through the drive-through. He left an extra $6.27 to pay for the car behind him and thought nothing of it. A week later, he learned from one of his old high school buddies that, after he left that day, each car paid for the car behind them, and this lasted for about 10 minutes.

Eduardo was ecstatic, and said, "I was 180% happier than I had ever been. I have never experienced such a valuable exercise as this."

This story has become part of nearly every talk I have given on random acts. It uplifts the participants and can be seen immediately on the faces of the audience—like an instant boost of calmness and peacefulness.

Eduardo's random acts did not end there. On St. Patrick's Day, he was driving to work at the restaurant to fill an extra shift, and all of the employees were dressed up. Eduardo described his outfit as a "pseudo Sadie Hawkins" style. He wore old suspenders with a hole and a patch on the right side, and a red bandana tied off to the left side. The straw hat was missing a few pieces and hung off the left side of his head. As he described his experience, we could almost imagine the cliché complete with a piece of straw dropped from the side of his mouth!

Eduardo was driving along when he saw an elderly couple pulled off on the side of the road, frantically trying to flag someone down. He watched as a number of cars passed by. He had been working out religiously on his weight and fitness training and realized that this could only help the couple in need.

He thought, "Doesn't anyone have any compassion in the world? I can't just drive past these folks. I would hate to think if they were my grandparents."

As he approached, the elderly woman blurted out, "Could you push the car to the side of the road? My husband has heart trouble, and I have trouble using this walker."

3

Eduardo agreed and began to push the vehicle off to the side of the road. The elderly couple offered to pay him $25 or treat him to a meal.

He gently replied, "No need. It was just a random act of kindness."

Eduardo walked away and felt better. Whenever I tell this story, the smile he brought to the couple's faces is transferred to my audience; I've seen their smiles and imagine a sparkle in their eyes in reaction to hearing this tale.

Another time, Eduardo was working as the front-door host in an upscale Claremont restaurant. A destitute-looking, 53-year-old man walked in with dirt caked on the front and back of his pants. His shoes and body odor reeked as if he had walked through cow manure, and his kids, nine and twelve, looked like they should have been referred to Child Protective Services. Their clothes were torn and held together with safety pins; their shoes were mismatched, and their hair was tied in knots. The father leaned forward to beg for food to feed his children.

Eduardo escorted the family out the door and said, "We don't feed the homeless."

As soon as these words left his mouth, Eduardo reflected on the class project of random acts of kindness. Moments later, he brought out complimentary hamburgers and milkshakes to feed the family with one condition: They must eat the food outside the front of the restaurant. The homeless-looking man graciously agreed, and his children began to devour the meal as soon as they got it. The restaurant owner heard of his employee Eduardo's action, and was so moved by this act that he decided to post a sign saying, "We now feed the homeless."

A week later, the gentleman returned in a Mercedes-Benz and dressed in an expensive suit, explaining that he wanted to teach his children to appreciate what they had in their home and not take things for granted. He made the announcement that he had started a foundation to serve the homeless, and he returned to express his gratitude.

Eduardo could hardly restrain himself in my classroom. It seemed that the question he'd asked six months earlier — "what will I do as my last random act at the end of the semester?"—had come full circle. He began with a stranger, moved to senior citizens, helped the homeless population, and then returned to serve the world through his job at his restaurant. One could see huge progress in his interpersonal skills, which are such a huge part of the hospitality industry and the business degree that he hopes to pursue following college.

Every time I give a talk and include these stories, it is amazing to see calmness and serenity spread across the room. Audience members are filled with joy and happiness—transformed as disbelief becomes amazement that these things do exist in our world.

Similarly, we can turn to our world's great leaders to see how they use conviction to draw in their audience. Every schoolchild is taught the words of Martin Luther King, Jr., American pastor, activist, humanitarian, and leader. During King's time, there was no Facebook, Twitter, or instant messaging. He was virtually unknown before his world-famous August 28, 1963 "I Have a Dream" speech. The candor and passion in his voice unified a nation as he encouraged all people, regardless of their skin color or background, to work together.

Likewise, on the other side of the city, by the ocean swells, another group of students was also doing their part to make connections. Marcus, an 18-year-old, had driven across town with some friends for a blues band performance and spent the night in a local hotel. One night, by chance, they decided to take their guitars into the lobby and play some tunes to help the hotel guest relax. They did not receive a discount from the hotel and their names were not on the marquee. They simply wanted to share a few chords on the guitar, which turned into melodies. They brightened up the hotel lobby. Human beings all have the desire to share become closer to others. The actions of these musicians ignited humming sounds and finger snapping among their audience.

Another 18-year-old named Nikita, shared her tale. While working as a volunteer at a local, inner-city youth shelter, she arrived one day and saw the kids out on the street. The adult employees were sprawled out in front of the television, watching a rented film. Nikita and her colleague Benita dug through the closets and found some deflated balls. They also bought art supplies to inspire the teens to make some classy key chains. Soon, the teens became physically active and, through the art project, they bonded with one another on an interpersonal level while sharing their inner problems and secrets.

These additional benefits were the secondary reward. The desire to perform 'good works' and help others is inborn. It helps you feel better and reduces stress and anxiety. Moreover, sharing stories with other feels good and becomes a win-win situation for all involved. Telling stories like this inspires others to go out and do kind deeds.

Chapter 2
Setbacks to Steps Forward

In life, we all experience setbacks. These setbacks do not define us, but what we do to step forward does. Do we let these setbacks stop us, or do we get creative and move forward?

For example, in 2011, I was teaching my students to expand their English language skills through volunteer work in a Service Learning program in their community. In celebration, a story was written on the success of the program and was published in a college newspaper. A few years passed, and these activities were discontinued despite the positive impact they had on the student's language skills and for the broader community. This past semester, a fellow faculty member found this old newspaper clipping and used it as a teaching tool to show his students the positive ideas that another instructor was using in her courses.

In one of my talks, "Setbacks to Steps Forward: How the Worst Year Became the Best Year of My Life," I told the story about how I had fractured my right hand on an extended weekend cruise. This happened just before starting the new term, and the school had pushed back the start date to aid in my recovery. On the first day, I walked into the classroom with a huge white cast in a 90-degree angle on my right arm. Need I mention that I am right-handed?

My message to the students was, "Don't mind the monstrosity on my arm. My mouth works, and my mind is in perfect condition to turn one of you into a speech champion in the campus competition in three months!"

I felt sure of my talent because I had coached high school decathlon champions several years earlier. The students stared back at me skeptically. Before I could teach them, I had to overcome my own fear of teaching with the handicap of using only my left hand. Research on positive psychology states that, if you set your mind on the end game and believe things are possible by acting as if they truly are, you can make them a reality. So, as the research predicted, the results were simply an execution of the formula of success: Teach it, tell it, and transpire it into reality.

The semester came to a conclusion, and nearly half the class came out to support the speech tournament in Ventura. My students, who began the term three weeks late, came in second and third place with cash prizes.

Later that night in class, it was hard to tell who was flying higher: myself or the students. One student came in with glowing tales of how pleased her parents were over her success. There were other students who observed the competition and wanted to protest the outcome based upon perceived improprieties in the selection of the first-place winner. I refocused their energies, saying that we had all achieved success. The underdog, unexpectedly, had come home delivering their well-deserved prize.

The story doesn't end there. The stage had been set, and I knew deep in my heart that the first-place winner was sitting in my classroom on the other side of town. The following week, I began my class with this motivating message:

"I have seen your talks and I know the first place winner is one of you sitting in this class. I know your talents, and I can see it happening in this class!"

The day of the competition came, and many students were there to watch history unfold. It was startling to hear the voices of student empowerment; my student was the best. She had intuitively recognized her potential for success with this challenging assignment. My college student had taken first place!

When you have self-confidence, you can share it with the world. Your positive energy draws in more positive energy to make miracles come to life and bring victory. It paralleled what another student had said as she reflected on her victory:

"The keys to success are putting myself—mind, body, and soul—in the character I am playing. By bringing that person to life, it helped me win first place!"

I tell this same story the first day of the semester, and my students' instant response is a huge round of applause when they hear my paths of victory story from the previous students. I can see the wonder in their eyes as they ask themselves, "Will it be me or you who will win?"

That was, by far, the best and most successful semester I had ever had up until then. It was not easy or fun writing with my left hand, but I turned the misfortune into a challenge to improve my handwriting. This was one small step that helped me get past all the negatives, the things I thought I couldn't do. I needed to focus my energies on the transformative process in order to help my students overcome their fears and learn the keys to becoming champions.

What initial disappointments have you faced in your life? Have you seen them change course over time? Is there someone with whom you could share your message of hope and encouragement?

Chapter 3
Improving Relationships with Hearts of Humanity

There's a certain power that comes from speaking your truth. Everyone has stories to tell with events and moments that have changed their lives forever. The creators of these stories were comprised of different ethnicities, representing the fabric of our society. At the younger end, there were my high school students, who grew up in the inner city. Their life stories were filled with tragedy, loss, and heartache that could truly break anyone's soul. Yet, through their struggles, they reached out for a connection to others.

These stories flow from my mind like wine poured from a carafe, and they bring back sweet memories of yesterday. Anita, who was a quiet, petite, fresh-faced 16-year-old girl, who dressed in the hottest fashions, told a tale of sorrow about how she lost her father, brother, and cousin to gang violence, and then her nephew to suicide—all in less than three months.

As Anita concluded these sad words, I sprang out of my seat, no longer just a college professor but a counselor.

It's truly heart-wrenching to hear the sadness that this young person has experienced in her life, but there is also a lesson that we can take with us: *Life is a precious commodity with no lifelong satisfaction or guarantee of happiness.* Realizing this, we can validate our existence with love. We need to communicate our affection for those who are close to us while we have the time. It's best to share words of hope and compassion with those whom we love, as if these words were our last.

I asked each student to take the time to share their deepest gratitude and connect with those who were close to them.

Amazingly, I thought to myself, "I can't ask my students to do what I will not do myself!"

I began by writing a letter of gratitude to my older sister Judy, but it coincided with tax season, so I am not sure what impact it made. Next was my brother Jerry, who is also an accountant, but his message was most surprising. He stopped what he was doing to say how much he had appreciated the memories I had brought forth, and how grateful he truly was for what I had done. I have never been that close with Jerry, so it came as quite a surprise. Then, my other sister Robin couldn't wait to call and engage me in a conversation, but sadly I was faced with complaining students at that moment. In reflection, it was amazing how all the words of love and admiration brought a connection to my life and to those of my students.

There were several students who felt empowered by my request to share their love with others. Remarkably, many teens, who were scared to share their intimate thoughts with their families, actually expressed their love to their parents for the first time in their lives. One 16-year-old named Alejandro recounted how his single dad played the role of both parents and how difficult it was to do that and hold down his job.

Today's teens are involved in their own world with school friends and families. Meanwhile, their internal cycles, including hormonal changes, force them to sleep in when they should be getting up. Yet, Alejandro had an appreciation for what his father did and managed to get up earlier, just to help out his father. There is nothing greater than feeling responsible for helping to bring a family closer together.

With wonder and awe, Alejandro's classmates glanced over to hear what their peer had said, and audience members in another venue dropped their jaws in amazement. The second response was gratitude that there may be hope left in the world.

Moving beyond high school, my international students are like a mini United Nations. Their connections took another form when a woman named Saniya, who migrated from Yemen, was pregnant with her second child. She described how she opened her home to a group of 24-year-old men, who migrated from her old country. They were feeling a bit homesick, so she cooked her country's favorite foods and invited these men to her home, which reminded them of their life back in Yemen. They certainly were far from home, but their taste buds carried them back to the hills of their native homeland. As Saniya shared her stories, other students reflected on the homelands they left with the new life they created, shedding tears and trying to wipe them away without the others noticing. The stories they shared reignited old emotions.

A beautiful Russian model named Tanya, with blond hair and blue-grey eyes, shared a method that she used to overcome her lonely days. She bought a bunch of daffodils, went to a popular shopping mall, and handed them out to each and every lady whom she passed along the way. With each flower she gave, it warmed her heart and took her mind beyond herself to that of giving to others.

By the end of the school term, students were asked to reflect on their favorite story, and Tanya's story—with a religious connection—was selected as one of the most popular. There is a saying in religious scriptures that God works in different ways. One way is to guide us in the act of giving, which helps to bring us eternal happiness. It is how we know that God is out there, working all around us.

In this process, students became more than bodies in a class, moving toward a larger goal of passing the course. Students became connected to one another through the stories containing random acts of kindness. For example, I had a student named Amanda, who struggled with low self-confidence and depression. Lucky for her that I had the watchful eye to see when she needed help. In response to my kindness, she used her interpersonal skills to reign in a rambunctious student named Alan. He had poor communication and coping skills but by working with him, she was able to help turn him around. As a result, the two became especially close friends.

Later during the term, Amanda needed to make up some lost points for missed class assignments and had to drive to Covina, which was one hour away. Based on her past performance, I was concerned whether it would be another no-show. In fact, I seriously doubted that she would show up at all. However, she came back in the company of her buddy Alan an hour late.

Seeing one missed opportunity, I found another chance to make up the points by competing at a local school. In order to ensure her participation, I asked her to arrive early. To my amazement, Amanda and Alan were both waiting when I arrived—an hour before the contest began! Given their history, it was a miracle that they waited so long. That day, Amanda gave one of her best talks, no doubt due to her punctuality and the supportiveness of her new friend, Alan.

I have never felt as much gratitude as I did from Amanda when she came to say goodbye and stated, "I am so glad that you helped me to save my life. I will never forget all that you have done on my behalf."

This became one of the proudest moments in all of my teaching career — on par with speaking from the TEDx stage. My greatest high is the TEDx talk titled "Language Comes to Life," where I take my students to the theater to learn English. It is monumental in my life telling the audience, and it also helps my students increase their understanding. Likewise, my audiences get the similar positive vibe when they hear me share my students' tales of saving lives and changing the world, each in his or her own way.

Throughout history, there are points of reflection on the world, such as when Franklin D. Roosevelt, in his April 14, 1938, Fireside Chat, stated, "I believe that we have been right in the course we have charted. To abandon our purpose of building a greater, a more stable and a more tolerant America would be to miss the tide and perhaps to miss the port. I propose to sail ahead. I feel sure that your hopes and I feel sure that your help are with me."

Roosevelt was unifying different parts of his constituents in a very difficult time. Like FDR, in helping one another, these students are healing themselves while unifying whole communities using the power of kindness. They are promoting the open expression of extraordinary gratitude through everyday exchanges.

A former ballerina named Juliet, who enrolled in my class, aspired to be a pediatrician. She shared the saga of a personal hardship with a rare disease, which took her out of ballet and required the care of a special doctor, who helped her regain her strength to learn to walk again. Juliet was also greatly influence by her grandfather, who was the head surgeon in the community in which she grew up. In gratitude of what she had received during her illness, she wanted to be a pediatrician and work with the underprivileged in order to give back to society for the time she had been cared for as a youngster. Juliet worked with the very young in a childcare center, and had the capacity and the heart to deal with older people at the end of their lives. Each of her stories opened our minds helped us to peer into the heart of humanity.

Juliet shared a story about one Valentine's Day at a bakery. A woman named Francesca, who was in front of her on line, was short of cash. Juliet offered the extra money needed to complete the transaction, enabling Francesca to buy a gift for her beloved. Later, the two women talked and Juliet heard Francesca's stories of the life she'd always wanted but could never achieve: being a professional ballerina. Each of Francesca's stories was another part that connected the human spirit.

Telling stories that reach the human heart is one of my greatest gifts, and it has played a role in many of my old battles. Many years ago in my teaching career, I was doing what I had always done: trying to help out those careless students who could never manage to get their work done. I offered extra credit if they would e-mail George W. Bush, the 43rd U.S. President, regarding their feelings about the upcoming war in Iraq, a war which was prompted by the search for weapons of mass destruction. As proof of having completed the assignment, I simply requested the automatic response that is generated when the public writes a message to an elected official, expressing their opinion regardless of their political leanings or position.

I expressed no bias as to whether they were for or against the war. Yet what I said was twisted as messages often are in the game of telephone. Unfortunately, the news spread like wildfire around my world. Rather than recognizing this as promotion of non-partisan, civic engagement, I was suddenly seen as an outcast as if dictating political preferences and my students' thoughts. I certainly didn't do so and this was never my intention, but that was what the media bought and sold.

Everywhere I turned, on every major radio and television station, another story of the radical life I lived and the activities of my spouse were drawn into the fray.

I was even put under the spotlight at one school, which asked, "Are you conducting similar activities in our school?"

Hardly so. For example, one student, a lieutenant who served at Camp Pendleton, sent off new recruits to fight the war. I always treated him with the utmost respect, but the accusations continued. Another school received calls from some "very conservative individuals," who attempted to have me barred from teaching at another campus.

I will never forget what the head of one union said: "You will never be let go from any of our schools as long as I am in this position."

The original school removed me from the classroom, and the case seemed bound for court but the night before my story aired with Connie Chung, Elizabeth Smart was kidnapped. Her tragedy took me out of the spotlight.

Painfully, five months later, my case was thrown from the court back into the hands of the mediator where I was finally able to offer my side of the story. I was trying to help my students and not harm them, but words and misbeliefs took center stage. Once my version of the story was finally heard, my passion—combined with compassion—soared;

the pauses pierced the air like popcorn popping. The nonverbal expression I saw in his eyes and body language reflected his unspoken words: He understood my position.

As we walked down the hall, and as the door closed with the mediator, my attorney said that he had never heard a client tell a better story to captivate hearts and minds as he did in hearing my side of the tale. The results were simple: I was vindicated and allowed to continue teaching but the world never got to hear the truth that I was found innocent.

Is this story, which was suppressed at the time, the reason I continue to speak today in order to share my message and reach the hearts and minds of my audience? If I was able to endure all of those hardships, imagine what you could do to triumphantly pass your story along to others! Each day, I stand in my classrooms around the world, giving people the tools they need to make the connections that count the most.

What are the connections that hold all of us together?

Are there people in our lives for whom we could take the time to open the lines of communication?

What messages do we need to share to help mitigate a painful past or strengthen our future ties with one another?

Chapter 4
A Flicker in the Heart

I know the work is complete when I feel a flicker in my heart. It lets me know that I am human. My eyes smile when I see the sparkle of recognition in the audience. We have connected. A grin goes from one side of my face to the other, a dawning joy spreads to every person in the room.

Here is one such story from Susie, a student who heard my talk on Blog Talk Radio. From the moment she heard it, she immediately decided that she wanted to make random acts of kindness a bigger part of her life.

At the end of every workday, Susie sees a homeless man named John sitting outside. She typically offers some spare change from her pocket or begins a conversation. On this particular day, Susie was really tired and cranky, but John asked her a question:

"Can I take a shower to feel human again?"

Suzie didn't think twice and paid his bus fare to ride across the city to her home. Once they entered Susie's apartment, she showed him the bathroom so he could clean up. Meanwhile, she prepared a care package of food and toiletries, including soap, deodorant, toothpaste, and a toothbrush. John thanked her for helping.

"I really felt terrific!"

After John left her home, Susie felt better than when she had left work.

She thought, "Homeless people are folks too, and helping out the less privileged brought me immense happiness."

She hoped that, in telling this story, it might influence someone else to do something nice for another person. As you read this story, what thoughts go through your head?

The next day in class, to my great surprise, Susie, in the middle of a speech, shared her own life, which had taken a similar turn. She had been homeless, and her house was replaced with the four wheels of an old beat-up Volkswagen Beetle. She told her classmates that it was her experience being homeless that enabled her to help John and other homeless people. Being homeless became the tool that taught her empathy, which later allowed her to give back to others. This is a common theme in most 12-step programs for recovering addicts from all walks of life. The greatest gift of recovery is returning the favor of kindness to someone else. We are all hard-wired to help others.

As I shared that story with a local service organization, one member described it as their favorite story. Each story cannot be told alone, they inspire and must be joined by another. We all collect stories. It is like our minds are recording devices that are stopped and restarted for each story that touches our hearts.

The next story was about a football player named Ryan, who told his troubles with a torn shoulder and neck injury from a scary concussion the previous weekend. This injury kept Ryan from the field he loved so much. His passion was deep. The value of football in his life was better than any relationship; it *was* his relationship.

As Ryan shared his pain, he expressed his sorrow as his heart cried out with these words:

"I need to be on that field."

His words evoked the passion of a Southern Baptist Minister quoting the Gospel and preaching from the Book of Revelations.

Ryan continued…

"My life and scholarship are on that field, and the coaches are keeping me from reaching my most important goal by holding me back from meeting the college recruiters, who are unable to see me in action on the field."

Ryan shared that he even had a doctor's note, which indicated that he didn't need to speak because of the stress it would create. Yet, he came to class, dressed the part in an outfit more suited for an interview or for being the best man in a wedding party. His passion matched mine when I profess the power of random acts of kindness.

His classmates listened intently, all eyes frozen on the athlete. They were enraptured, recalling their own athletic feats when they had broken a bone, lost a title, or missed out on some other major accomplishment in their life. Their heads were cast downward, as if in the silent internal dialogue of the Serenity Prayer:

*God, grant me the serenity to accept the things I
cannot change,
"The courage to change the things I can,
And wisdom to know the difference.*

As Ryan told his tale, my sixth personality profile emerged, as if I had been dialed up and called to report to duty. This commentary was titled, "The Dangers and Problems of Concussions." I played the role of psychologist and the humanist side of a doctor, begging him to give his body the chance to rebuild and recover.

"Do you know the number of young people who lose their lives on the field at the young age of 20 or less? Do you want to live a short life, lose everything, and simply become another statistic?"

Life is about choosing a path to follow. As I stated these warnings, pictures passed through my mind of other folks who were not so lucky and of the pain they suffered because they were too impatient to let their body have its time.

It reminded me of my fractured wrist and how stifled I felt at home prior to the start of a new semester and a new school. I was unable to dress myself or drive, but my mouth worked just fine. I too had to wait for the clock of time and doctor's note of approval to give me the eventual okay to return to work.

Later that day, while returning to West Los Angeles to teach my high school class, another student named Pablo had a similar story, but his injury was about a broken finger.

He described fighting through the pain to hopefully win the scoring touchdown and win the playoff.

Once again, as I told the story of my fractured wrist, my tears were not released for the pain but, for the fact that if I hadn't allowed my hand to repair, the injury could have followed me for the rest of my life. It could have prevented the full use of my right hand, which helps me write. When we are young, we think we are unbreakable, but we must realize that there is a reason that we experience pain: It is a sign that we must listen to our body's warnings.

Upon leaving my class, one of my students shouted, "You are not just Professor Kahn. You are Mama Kahn!"

I have always said, "I have no children—just dogs at home—so my students are my children!"

Each story I tell convinces the listener to add one of their own. My favorite message is, "We never know the impact that our stories may have on another person's life." I recently attended a networking meeting and, while waiting in line, met a lady named Candace, who was due to give a brief introduction and give an award to Jan Perry, a municipal politician who was working under Mayor Eric Garcetti. I could see from Candace's body posture that her nerves and anxiety about speaking were as tightly wound as my students on the first day of class. I shared my pearls of wisdom to match the ones Candace wore around her neck.

"Just focus on the message you experience, and the words will simply flow."

Following my script, she got up with the same girlish laughter and, once the story began, the rest just flowed. If we tell our stories and let the words percolate, they simply emerge like pure water from an artesian spring.

Similarly, no one can forget the wisdom of Steve Jobs, American entrepreneur, marketer, and inventor. His speech covered three stories, connect the dots, follow the passion, and find the love that keeps it together. In 2005, Jobs gave a commencement address at Stanford University and shared his life through stories. As he spoke the words, he wove an invisible web of emotion that touched everyone present that day. Each time I listen to his story, his words form a bond of human connection; we can see ourselves in the same situations. We have all struggled to find our path when a mismatch of expectations and life's actual experiences shake us to our core.

Jobs' next story has been part of every motivational speaker's message since the birth of time: Find and follow your passion, and life will lead you to success. Jobs discovered this through myriad transactions with different worlds.

I see a parallel in my own stories—of traveling the world in an international entertainment organization, pursuing a career in media while selling commercial air time, moving into corporate and classroom training, and expanding my messages to the word. I too have moved back and forth from broad-targeted messages to small ones.

Finally, the last part of Jobs' story is about finding the love that keeps it together. Each time I read and listen to his words, they bring out the floodgates of an emotional wall of tears. I know that I am not alone because, when I share these words with others—even with those for whom English is their second language—the response is always the same. It is true magnificence.

In the same vein, as I begin each day by sharing a part of my world with my students and with the organizations with which I work, my stories have an equally valid point: They bring out emotions that touch the soul and strike a chord. You can't sit through these stories and be untouched. People are driven to share their own acts, or they feel inspired to go out and take some action of their own. Furthermore, I have found that, in telling these stories, a movement and a following have emerged where the heart guides the love from one realm to the next. Students and businesspeople will go miles just to experience part of the excitement.

What stories do you tell in your life that are missing key segments?

Are you holding yourself back from telling stories and withholding critical information that, if told, might help others move forward in their lives?

What are you waiting for?

There are no guarantees for our time on this planet, and the present is the best we have to make it happen.

Chapter 5
From Despair to Repair

You may think that the recipient of a random act of kindness would be the primary beneficiary; however, many times the true receiver is the giver. I hear this over and over from individuals who are, by all of society's standards, highly successful. They have great jobs, nice homes, and healthy families, but still they feel empty, like something inside of them is missing. They are walking through the world feeling disconnected or in despair.

Take Jamie, a fellow participant in a business training seminar I attended. He shared a story that reminded me of the impact that giving can have on both parties:

"I am pretty successful in my sales career and, every once in a while, I will treat a homeless person to share a meal. I learn the most incredible things while chatting with these people, who may be brilliant beyond years. Yet, at some point in their life, they got on the wrong track and have found themselves without a home. These stories give value to my life and make it whole. It completes the whole picture."

Jamie also shared the value of spending time with our youth, who were also participants in this seminar. It is startling to tap into our youth. Our cluttered world causes us to close the windows of our minds, preventing us from seeing young people's value and contributions. The creativity and imagination that youth brings offer new clarity to our world of possibilities.

Recently, I met a gentlemen name Avo, who used to live on the street with no more than a penny to his name. Through the chance of a miracle, he was able to pull himself out of despair to a much better place where knowledge and skill worked to his advantage. Once he set his mind toward success - the sky was the limit. He used his firsthand experience of nothingness to help businesspeople create wealth and life satisfaction. Yet, once again, he reached this peak in incredible wonderment, and decided to pull back to a simpler path and enjoy life's more beautiful moments of sunrises and sunsets. During his break, he was awakened by a call from his conscience urging him to spread his wings and fly to international crisis zones. Once there, he would use his connections from around the world to offer the needy access to medical supplies.

While in Guayaquil, Ecuador, another person named Gary found his path through the study and cultivation of plants for natural remedies indigenous to the area when he noticed the poor condition of Guayaquil's elementary school. Forty-two students in first- through sixth-grade, were crammed into one tiny room. They were forced to share limited supplies and sit at broken tables while their volunteer teacher gave lessons on a damaged chalkboard. Gary set up a foundation and has just completed the construction of their new school, which already has 119 students. The school continues to grow and become a place where they may educate Ecuador's future leaders.

Ruiz owns a company that does work in the African sub-Saharan desert, where most villagers earn less than 25 cents a day. His company uses the area to mine for precious fluids only found in this region. On a business trip, one of his vendors suddenly saw beyond his product, and realizing the disparity between the people's poverty and his company's profits, he began to create a school that would become a window of hope and opportunity.

It is amazing to see the process wherein seeming nothingness can create a well of hope and dreams. It opens a new door, which moves personal pain and suffering aside, to a new arena, while offering hope and inspiration to other travelers, both far and near.

In the span of one weekend, synchronicity seemingly encountered these phenomenal individuals, who were each creating a legacy through their endeavors. There is a saying that, when you put out your dreams to the world, you will be blessed in return with astonishing rewards. I have my own vision, one of transforming the world through the action of my students' stories.

There is no greater joy in teaching than to see the impact that one creates by simply asking a mere question: "What simple changes would you make in your life to become a better person"? The answers below tell volumes about what our future world may look like.

Annabellina, a 17-year-old Colombian, who came from a downtrodden inner city high school, described a "1% change" to stop letting things bother or annoy her so quickly (for example, when someone does not know how to use the proper "your" and "you're".) Making this simple change benefits her positively because she becomes more accepting toward other people's flaws. Everyone has their own flaws and, when I do not accept others' flaws, that's a flaw in itself. This is the "1% change" that Annabellina would make.

How much would it improve each of our lives by reading the principles and applying them to our own lives? So much money, time, and energy are used in therapy, programs, and beyond just to get us to understand these simple lessons. It is even more incredible when the words come from a teenager. How might our world shift if we gave some power to our youth to impact their world?

Tazania, a 23-year-old, a slender and petite woman, wrote that her family lived in Los Angeles in a small Kyrgyz community, whose residents all came from the same town in Central Asia. Most of them were young males, and they had to share rooms to save money. She felt badly for them because they didn't know how to cook meals.

Tazania explained, "In our culture, boys are not allowed to be in the kitchen. It's bad for them, and I don't like it. They always ask other girls from our country to cook our traditional food, but girls don't have time to cook. They work, and some of them don't like to cook. I decided to cook for them. My husband and I invited them to our condominium for dinner. Six boys came. They were so happy and ate their meal with joy. I felt so happy that we could do something special for our community."

Nigela, a pregnant Nigerian woman, recognized the importance of sharing what she could not use on her own. She has a huge heart but she was financially strapped and on surviving on food stamps. Each week, she would collect her box of food staples and bring it back to her home. When others select food for someone, the people receiving it, although grateful, will find food they love and that which they would rather leave behind. Nigela decided that the excess food she received had no place in her home, and she would rather take what she wouldn't use to people living on the streets who had no food at all. The core values of her heart, always focused outward, helped her to see how she could brighten up someone else's world.

The monetary value may be small, but the magnitude of helping others goes quite far.

Other students would show up to help, and they were truly miracle workers on a mission from somewhere special. The semester emerged as a war of words that appeared before my eyes.

No matter how bad the world might seem, there was still a rainbow of kindness that came forth ... or so it seemed.

The semester was drawing to a close, and my enthusiasm was building every day with the potential to publish a book and sell it to college students. When I approached the ranking official's office, he welcomed me with a smile that didn't need explanation. He had already read the same chapter the president had read and loved and knew the greatness that lay inside.

He explained, "It will only be a short time before the bureaucrats give their blessing."

It was like a mere rubber stamp, which would only take a few days.

Days became weeks, and the clock of the semester was quickly coming to an end. Just like a good screenplay, the weeks were running short, and I suddenly came home to find a desperate message on my answering machine from a hospital bed.

My approval had been rejected and, for the second time in the term, I was given a warning or a lesson to learn. My students could tell their stories in class, but they could not be used in any other way.

I felt as if my heart had been struck by an arrow and all the goodness and glamour had been struck down. I wallowed in darkness. I later spoke to a few close friends. Their advice was to repeat the adage, "When one door closes, another opens." Living in a solitary world with my vision, it felt as if the candle illuminating my path forward had been extinguished.

Yet, through the external power of social support, I began to hear another voice that is a critical part of who I am: "Don't quit. If it doesn't work this way, I will find another way. I will open a new door and expand my vision beyond the wall of my classroom in different parts of the city and even to the wider world."

Here is what I posted on my blog on that dark and dreary day— May 11, 2012—as the sun began to show a glimmer of hope through the darkness:

"Recently, I learned some heart-wrenching news that temporarily limited my focus. I went to sleep on the bad news and proceeded to launch the expansion of my blog from the classroom to the universe. If, in reading my stories, it has inspired you to do something nice for others, let me know.

"Last week, I attended Maurice De Mino Boot Camp. Maurice has presented before with internationally recognized speakers such as Les Brown and Mark Victor Hansen. In the workshop, I learned the wording of my company goal: 'Master the Message with Passion and Purpose.' I returned to my classroom and had my students vote on how they perceived my company's message. The response was phenomenal. Nearly all of my students agreed that this is what I do in my classroom, and this should be the message that I share with the world.

"In compiling the stories for this blog, I would like to express my gratitude beyond words for the people who have aided in this process. A fellow colleague, who works at one of my institutions, offered to help me type the stories listed here. Another faculty member at another institution expedited the process by scanning the documents and converting them to Microsoft Word documents. A fellow senior citizen, who became my friend when I fractured my wrist, is editing my work. While discovering the need for a more attractive logo, another colleague whom I know through work, offered their assistance as well, to soothe my pain.

"The world is filled with nice people. It is disheartening how society tends to shut out good news, when they are worried about who may be offended and turn to potential lawsuits. Studies show that good news publications go out of business. Yet, they are replaced with front-page stories of terrorist attacks, school violence, bombings, fires, kidnappings, and rapes. There are no limits on when it comes to running bad news.

"It is my vision to create a place where people can share the incidents of good things that happen in their world. Just this morning, I spoke with four friends. One friend had helped a person with housing, another shares her leftovers with the homeless, a third helps kids with sports, and another donates time to the elderly.

"I am certain that there is something that everyone is doing that is worth sharing. Please help me promote the positive work that each of us is doing, regardless of your age, classification, or setting. I look forward to hearing your suggestions."

Once again, just four months into the process, my body was internalizing the message. I knew from day one that there was magic being unraveled. Even though my daytime world tried to extinguish the flame, the message burned brightly in all the groups at which I spoke and shared the stories.

A member at a local service organization in San Fernando still raves about one of the first speeches I gave. A local college trustee reminds me each time we meet that people were flattered and touched by the presentation that began my talk on random acts of kindness. This first group became a springboard to the whole world of this service organization. Since that initial engagement, I have spoken at nine groups and delivered a keynote address to their club.

Yet, for every success, there was also the counterbalance of the other side of life. I was great at engaging groups to get me to speak. It truly nourished my soul and made me reach the highest level of self-actualization by doing what I was born to do and seeing the responses in the faces of my adult audiences. The other side included vendors and students, who would offer some help and the best plate of goods or services. No sooner was the plate of goods offered than it vanished into thin air, as if it never existed.

I had a colleague, who came with high credentials. My expertise is in oral communication, but I always go to my pool of resources for the technological realm. Unfortunately, the first change to my web page was the equivalent of a national disaster.

I was elated that I had fine-tuned my message, but my online presence looked like a grade-school project. Besides teaching during the day, I was scrambling to find a resolution to pull me out and replace this horrible embarrassment.

A short time later, I found a friend who said that they would come to my rescue with a limited amount of time, just to get me out of the dangerous forest of humiliation. If only I had listened to the advice given at my recent workshop: "Don't hire a friend or family member to help you in your business."

The initial draft on my web page got rave reviews, and we were off to a good start. Yet, once that image took ground, a wall of inconsistency formed.

I would call and ask, "Can you help me out? I need to make some changes."

Their response was sporadic at best. This created an enormous amount of frustration where I was constantly looking for a replacement, but what I found was an amazing lesson or phenomenon about web programmers, similar to used-car salespeople: They promise the world, and the realty of when it will happen or how much it will cost is an entirely different perspective than the original offer.

Many of the vendors I used could fill hundreds of pages of turmoil in another book. Yet, each sad story of the daily grind of getting the webpage done was counterbalanced by the wonderment of what my incredible students had done to improve the world. They helped me in my business world, and their activities helped bolster my mental state.

A pregnant student named Natana worked for the disabled and had to stop due to her health; however, she decided to go back one day to make some soup and spend the day. She shared a story about her client, who was very pleased:

"I can hardly ask anyone for help; it is just beyond who I am. Your simply being here is the answer to all my dreams."

Natana helped straighten up the workspace. As she left, she stood outside for a few moments to shed some tears.

"Why is the world so inconsiderate of the disabled and unwilling to offer their time or space? Why must the busy people become overburdened to share their limited time?"

As the words left Natana's mouth, you could hear and see many sighs and smiles in those classmates who joined her circle. Their eyes seemed to express disbelief about the story she shared.

More incredulous is that this is the same student who I turned to if I needed to get something done, such as videotaping a speech, taking some photos, and following through. Natana would never let me down.

The message also created a healing element. At one point in the term, conflict had arisen over disgruntled students who claimed that they weren't learning, yet the proliferation of stories—sharing and reviewing what had been learned each day—that had enabled us to persevere.

At the semester's end, these students were surveyed and asked if they saw the value of these random acts of kindness.

They resoundingly said, "Yes!"

They were also asked if they would continue to do them after the term, and every student in every place I taught agreed that this would continue well beyond the class.

After five months of service, and continued interaction with the stories as told by my students and as transmitted in my speeches, I began to experience an internal shift as a person. A shift also appeared in feedback from my students and groups to whom I presented. The message was sticking. People were not simply hearing but were processing and retaining the information for months afterward.

One student said, at the semester's end, that the completion of the random acts had taken her out of the shell of shyness and, in giving to others, she became a different person who was more concerned with others' well-being.

Another group I'd addressed became the seed to open doors of inspiration, taking my public speaking ambition into a reality. The memories of my talk still exist as brightly as yesterday. As I move my talks into a new generation, they are opening the doors of opportunity and allowing me to share the steps of my business success.

Every day in my class, I share a story of random acts of kindness. It begins with one story, which becomes a seed that opens the heart and brings other receptivity into focus.

A pregnant, 22-year-old, international student named Margie, claimed, "I always do for others, and no one does anything for me. I am tired of always giving. It is my time to receive."

One day, she left her house to shop and fill her belly. Her basket was overflowing and, when she got to the register, she learned that her bill was $25 and thought that she had only $10. She started to put back food to get it down to the amount in her wallet. Suddenly, she found no money in her wallet and realized that she'd have to leave empty handed.

No sooner was she considering leaving when another customer in line walked over and said, "Here. Let me pay for your groceries!"

She was in momentary disbelief and turned down the lady's offer. The woman insisted, and Margie walked out with $25 worth of groceries.

She thought, "Isn't it amazing that, when we do for others, there is someone who is taking care of us?"

After telling this story to each of my classes, I ask, "What do you think, and how does it make you feel? Do you feel the beat in your heart? Can you feel the change?"

Gender makes no difference as I hear my students' responses:

"That story is amazing! It makes me feel so good. It's sweet."

In each situation, yet another student was compelled to share their version of a random act of kindness. By the end of one day, a youngster named José in the high school class told his story of being at a supermarket. When an older lady dropped all of her groceries, and they had rolled all around the floor, everyone simply walked by, unfettered by the food around their feet. José took the time to collect the groceries and return them to the owner.

In return, he was rewarded with, "Thanks, young man. You made my day!"

During one class, I told my students that they would be giving a talk on the following day in response to a question that I would ask. That night, my students left panicked phone messages about what they were going to do the next day without prior preparation. I shared how easy it was to give a talk by speaking off the cuff. I told them not to worry, as they had a lifetime of experience to fill the prescription and answer any question that came their way.

Scholastic success has overflowed to my public presentations, and every talk comes back with even greater claims of gratitude and amazement. For example, I coached a client from a major, upscale restaurant chain, who spoke of my success in coaching his delivery: "That talk will go down in history as the best one I've ever given."

Sharing the success of this event has spawned more affection in other meetings where busy people, including accountants who are fighting the September 15th extension, find the time to say, "I wanted to let you know that your introduction at the table breathes success and optimism. I know that you touched and made an impact on every one at the table."

Better yet, the guest of honor, who is a former candidate for Los Angeles City Mayor, heard about my work with random acts of kindness and declared, "I believe that the city needs to hear more of your message."

Can it get any better than this?

Days later, I was conversing with a Florida businessman, who helps people with their webpages. I shared two success stories, and he was drawn under my wing; he offered to help me on my mission to spread the word and potentially allow me to help him craft his own message as well.

I came home, feeling more beat up than a dead doorbell, but this message radiated from my heart: "You must put me down on paper. I need to tell the world the miracle I am creating in the world around me."

Recently, I have been contacted by people of different faiths, who have offered a window of possibility to promote the words of another religious philosophy. We may not pray to the same being, but the messages we carry bring out the same response. Every major religion offers the premise that through aiding the less fortunate, the helper will be blessed as well.

Likewise, another coach, who does Tony Hsieh's blog for *Delivering Happiness*, inspired my beginning and offered the Prayer of Jabez, which essentially thanks the Mighty Creator and asks for His support as we reach to serve the higher good. It projects that, if we make a habit of expressing our praise, amazing things will come our way. Similar to Stephen Covey's *7 Habits of Highly Effective People,* if you put enough deposits into each of the characteristics, you will reap the rewards of balancing your account.

Shawn Anchor, American educator, author, and speaker, makes the case that, if you express gratitude every day for three acts of kindness, and write down two minutes of some unique experience that changed your day, and then combine it with meditation, you will be repaired. This story is best illustrated in my talk on "Reducing Stress with Random Acts of Kindness." In preparation for the talk, I realized that I couldn't give a speech unless I had total confidence and clarity with the issues I was addressing. I am usually stressed out for one reason or another, but this time I experienced a new high for this performance.

In an introductory exercise, one student wrote that he was concerned about his mental stability and couldn't promise what he may or may not do. I had never been as worried for my life as I was while reading those words. During the week that I gave my speech, I was under police protection, just in case the student decided to follow through.

I am very disciplined and sat down to write my speech. I sat in my favorite chair and let my mind wander.

"Didn't I do enough random acts? Were they going to protect me, or would I be the seventh tragedy on a college campus in 2013?"

Research from Shawn Anchor says that it takes just 20 seconds to change a mindset. So, I reminded myself to simply highlight the articles for my talk. As my highlighter pen touched the paper, I felt my mind shift from despair to repair. I was suddenly back in the saddle of pushing ahead with my dream.

It was like being struck by lightning. I had seen the power of shifting one's mindset. I immediately wanted to share it with someone else. Once I finished my talk, I celebrated by writing a letter to a person in trouble and sharing this major breakthrough. This message became my mantra: "Master the Message with Passion and Purpose. I am your inner guide to helping you reach your highest potential."

Research and transcendentalism has my back. If we work through our pain and unravel the past, we can learn to transform the negative lessons into positive moments of growth and inspiration. We don't deny the bad; rather, the negative commotion is a window for a new opportunity.

Once you change your perspective, the world takes on a new vision and opens up to you. As I have grown into the power of persuasion of helping move my audience, I too have grown to discover my own mission: "Help people reach the highest potential to be the best they can be!"

As John F. Kennedy, 35th U.S. President, stated during the Cuban missile crisis, which was a 13-day confrontation in October 1962 between the Soviet Union and Cuba on one side and the United States on the other, "No one can foresee precisely what course it will take or what costs or casualties will be incurred. ... the greatest danger of all would be to do nothing."

In my opinion, Kennedy is speaking to the Cuban people and explaining why his country is taking this effort. He recognized the huge danger and difficulties with the full knowledge that no one can know the loss of life that would occur, yet the requirements are sacrifice and self-discipline in the dangerous times ahead.

Everyone has approached a block with something they have desperately wanted to pursue and, through no fault of their own, been blocked out. What has been that block for you? How were you were able to overcome it and reach success?

In my world, it is a matter of precise focus and follow through. Set your eyes on the mission, persevere, and charge onward. I believe that, if there is a will, the way will eventually emerge or an alternative path will be revealed.

Chapter 6
Inspiration at Home and Abroad

Once you open your heart and begin to walk the pay-it-forward path, you will live your life that way. You will become addicted to magic and constant happy surprises, which seem to come out of nowhere. This book was inspired by all of those people who are doing amazing work and leaving a lasting legacy of connection and compassion.

Not too long ago, I harnessed a vision. I had a conviction that I wanted to write a transformational story through random acts of kindness. In reality, the process of initiation was almost a year when I started gathering the messages. After I began, I knew that I had an idea worth spreading.

Once the stories left the paper, enhanced by more and more human interaction, the force of a rocket booster ignited within, propelling me forward as my drive and determination continued to grow. I had a vision or a dream of being a professional speaker. Now, 35 speeches later, I have made connections with people and am doing that which my heart declares from the content of my stories and more. The momentum grows as the confidence I bring to each of my events, breeds even greater success. I can't find enough stages on which to share my contribution with the world.

The most amazing part of my story are the strangers who come to me, saying that they know or have heard about me. This summer, I entered a new class on the first day, told my students that I have this amazing project on random acts of kindness, and one of them said, "I have been following you for six months on Tumblr!" I had no idea I was even there.

When I began the next session, my new classes attracted more students than ever before. With the mere mention that I was a TEDx speaker—a program designed to give communities, organizations, and individuals the opportunity to stimulate dialogue through TED-like experiences at the local level—and a professor, the howls could be heard down the hall.

I originally began to the process as a tool to retain students; one section still has 33 of the 36 enrolled and other classes have similar numbers. Continuous enrollment is high as a result of using personal engagement. My students have been thrilled to learn skills and obtain examples that inspire better behavior and healthier attitudes.

Another student told me, "I have never had a teacher who inspired me as much as you did on the very first day of class."

The same individual decided to expand his horizon by coming out to record a later talk.

Soon, he introduced a new audience with which to share the daily successes of my own support network. Each week begins new chapter to write and record. I have found that, in each class, we begin with an exchange of a story from someone's personal life. From that single story, it grows to create an opportunity for transformational experiences that touch many other lives.

Recently, my goal was to develop a workshop for teaching how to give a talk without prior preparation. I began the class by asking who had an interaction using random acts. Kelly shared a story about how, at her job at Starbucks, she had found a local homeless man outside the door. Before her shift began, she brought out a donut and a cup of coffee.

Upon returning inside, her boss complained, "This should stop. We will never be able to turn people away."

Kelly responded, "I did not have my uniform on and yet, in my heart, I knew that I was doing the right thing."

Once more, I was sharing this story and taking in the new stories that these students in another class had shared.

Once more, I polled the audience and asked, "How many of you feel better than when you walked in today?"

The hands went up in the same way as they do with my audiences throughout the community. I am at the beginning of creating a legacy I can feel proud to leave behind when I depart from this world.

Many students say, "Where is your next event?"

When I tell them, they say, "It's too far. I can't go there. If you find a place and make me the speaker, I will come."

To my surprise, Annabellina, the 17-year-old Colombian woman whom I talked about earlier, approached me with a story about Sergio Garcia, the Mexican-born immigrant who is fighting in the California Supreme Court to practice law for which he was trained in Mexico.

The student returned after break, and said, "Here, teacher. Call this number. He wants to speak with you."

Several hours later, I had a potential engagement in Chico, helping to raise money for a brand new foundation to help students afford their education.

Days earlier, another student named Brigita commented on the successful outcome of her speech. Her mom, who is also a professional speaker, helped her.

My student said, "I can't wait to tell my mom!"

I asked, "What type of company does she work for?"

"They manufacture food products."

"Great! Where is the company?"

She replied, "Back in Slovenia. Let me chat with her. If you come to Slovenia, we have a really big home you could stay at!"

"Where is Slovenia?"

"A small country in southern Central Europe, next to Italy."

I have always wanted to visit Italy! Wow, speaking internationally in Slovenia—that would be beyond my wildest dreams. Then in January I plan to travel there.

This reminds me of the February 4, 1916, Mahatma Gandhi speech at Banaras Hindu University. The situation was fraught with conflict and emotion, as the opposing side had been put into power.

He said, "But I do venture to suggest to you that we have now reached almost the end of our resources in speech-making; it is not enough that our ears are feasted, that our eyes are feasted, but it is necessary that our hearts have got to be touched and that our hands and feet have got to be moved."

Gandhi's words parallel my existence in professing the words and power of doing random acts of kindness. Most of my speeches end with the question, "Now that you have heard these stories, what does it remind you of? What acts have you seen or been the recipient of?" Moreover, the greatest gift is to inspire others to continue doing random acts, making our planet an even better place.

Every day, I make a new discovery. It seems that, whenever I come to the end of my list of speaking presentations, I have a burning desire to do more. These stories need to be told. When I share bits and pieces with the community, busy people make the time to come out and hear them, and I know that they have been touched.

Every day, I am blessed with another gift. I recently began my Friday teaching and, once again, we heard the horrors of new immigrants, the tragedy of heart disease, and stories about how to do the impossible—all coming from every corner of the world and represented by the people in my class.

Time had run out, and my assignment was as follows:

"The stories we heard today are better than any therapy session. I want you to consider your favorite one and, this week—when life gets tough, ugly, and frustrating—bring back that memory and focus on the story that brought you the greatest joy and put that huge smile to your face today."

I know the magic that is created every day. I tell a story, and the words create an internal reaction, bringing calm and serenity to the listener. This is more helpful than reading the newspaper because their new-found confidence bursts forth from inside. We all have a message and many stories that we want to share with the world.

As another semester drew to a close, an Armenian lady named Lisidea shared her Thanksgiving story. One day, she went to her closet and took out all of the excess that was not needed. Lisidea went to the street and gave these clothes to homeless people. Feeling very good, she came home to cook the Thanksgiving goods but, instead of putting them on the table, she packed the food in containers and distributed it to other homeless people. She will never forget the smiles on their faces. When Lisidea got home, she found a hospital on the Internet in need of blood donations, and she want there. It made her a bit light-headed but, in her heart, she knew that her blood was had the potential to save another's life.

In telling this story, Lisidea made the decision that these random acts were going to be a part of her life forever. Then, every other student's hand was raised, just like last semester. All of these students would carry on the tradition of random acts of kindness well beyond the class!

Epilogue
"What If?"

All of us have a space in our heart for something we care about and want to share. What is the fingerprint you want to leave on the world?

It is your turn to take that passion and come up with your own conviction. We are all consumed with our everyday existence and rarely take the time to listen to our inner voice that says, "What if?"

I challenge you to stop running. Take note of what is in your heart and put it on paper. We only live once, and your written words will be a record of how people remember you. Take the time and write down just a few words today; then, come back tomorrow and add to what you had before. Great orators or writers don't just fall from the sky. These are skills that are built over time, like any trade practiced by expert craftsman. Clarity in speech or writing will only come with continued practice.

What is your story?

What have you done?

Whose lives have you touched?

A colleague of mine said that the greatest tragedy of our lives may come from going to the grave with your story still inside of you. I have given you the formula to take a message and turn it into a movement. I have shown what you need to do.

What is stopping you from making your lasting impression on the world?

What is the story you will tell to touch hearts and create connections for a happier life?

Resources

National High School Decathlon Champions
at Taft High School

Language Comes to Life
TedX Conejo
http://youtu.be/9947cfXMhi4

www.lorildixon.com

www.rosalynkahn.com

The Elizabeth Smart Kidnapping
http://en.wikipedia.org/wiki/Elizabeth_Smart_kidnapping

Love It Forward
Over 100 Acts of Kindness article
(front and back) including organization info
http://gallery.mailchimp.com/1c6fc718f572962399a45423
b/files/Love_It_Forward_Event.1.pdf

Living Well Talk Radio
Suzanne Strowser and Kathleen O'Keefe-Kanavos
http://www.blogtalkradio.com/living-well-talk-radio/2013/09/04/your-life-purpose-revealed-tarot-runes

Ageless Living Lifestyle
Rigo Caveglia
http://www.blogtalkradio.com/thrivetalkradio/2013/10/12/how-random-acts-of-kindness-can-change-your-world

Diamond Healing Radio
Anastatia Chopelas Diamond Healing Radio
http://diamondhealingradio.com/rosalyn-kahn-professor-and-speaker/ 1-19-14

Ageless Living Lifestyle Rigo Caveglia

The Good Goodbye
Gail Rubin 2-17-14
http://agoodgoodbye.com/a-good-goodbye-radio/what-makes-an-obituary-go-viral-and-a-eulogy-memorable/

"Breakthrough Directions -
From Relationship Marketing To Business Success
Linda Feinholtz
http://www.BlogTalkRadio.com/jvqueen. April 15, 2014

Made in the USA
Charleston, SC
10 June 2014